Make Your Monster

Contents

Sue Whiting

RIGBY

Make a Monster

It's easy to make a monster.
This book tells you how.

glue

paints paint brushes

Materials:

scouring pad

2 plastic cups

2 buttons

cotton wool

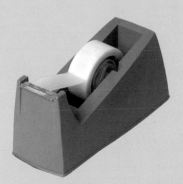
stickytape

2 boxes

coloured card

3

Monster Body

1 First make the body and the head.

- Use the big box to make the body.
- Tape the flaps together to make the box strong.

- Use the small box to make the head.
- Glue the small box to the top of the body.

Monster Eyes and Hair

2 Then make the eyes and the hair.

- Glue the buttons on the front of the head to make the eyes.

• Glue the cotton wool onto the top of the head to make the hair.

Monster Ears and Nose

3 Then make the ears and the nose.

- Stick a cup to each side of the head to make the ears.

• Stick the scouring pad on the front of the head to make the nose.

Monster Eyebrows

4 Now add the monster's eyebrows.

- Draw two triangles on some card.
- Cut them out and paint them.

Monster Mouth

5 Then make the monster's mouth.

- Draw the mouth on some card.
- Cut it out and paint the teeth.

Decorate Your Monster

6 Finally, decorate the monster's body.

- Use the card and your paints to make two hands.

• Make two feet.

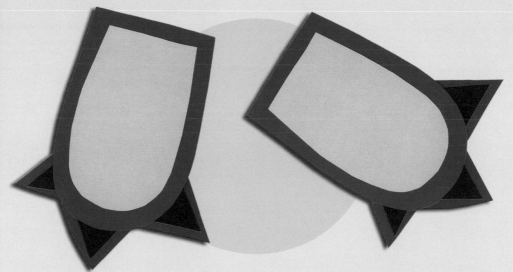

• Use the card and paints to also make some 'clothes' for your monster.

Finish Your Monster

- Glue the hands, feet and clothes to the front of the body.

Well done! You've made a monster

Other Monsters

What other monsters could you make?

Rigby, Halley Court, Jordan Hill, Oxford, OX2 8EJ
a division of Harcourt Education Ltd
www.myprimary.co.uk
Help and solutions for teachers plus the widest range of education solutions

Rigby is a registered trademark of Harcourt Education Ltd

0 433 07313 6 / 978 0433 07313 0 Make Your Own Monster Guided Reading Pack
09 08 07 06
10 9 8 7 6 5 4 3 2

Acknowledgements:
The author and publisher would like to thank the following for granting permission to reproduce
copyright material in this book:

Photographs: National Geographic p.4-5, p.6-7, p.8-9, p.10-11, p.12-13, p.15; Harcourt Education Ltd p.2,
(right and top left), p.3 (top, top right, middle right, bottom right); IStockPhoto p.3 (middle left); Getty
Imagesp.3 (bottom left).

Every effort has been made to trace and acknowledge copyright. The author and publisher would
welcome any information from people who believe they own copyright to material in this book.

Designed by Emma DeBanks
Project Manager: Sarah Eason
Consultant: Monica Hughes

Printed in China by China Translation & Printing Services Ltd.